STOCK MARKET
INVESTING
STRATEGIES

The Ultimate Guide to Learning and
Recognizing the Factors that Affect the
Stock Market. Discover How to Apply the
Best Profitable Strategies in the Active and
Passive Stock Market Without Fear.

DAVE ROBERT WARREN GRAHAM

 IPH BOOKS
INVESTING AND TRADING ACADEMY

"All investors have weaknesses and strengths. Some can win, some can lose. As long as you stick to your style, you can take advantage of both the good and the bad."

I dedicate this sentence and this book to all of you. Having your trading style and bringing out your strengths is important to be successful in investing. If you are at the beginning you will understand what they are! With this book, you will understand which strategies you can follow and integrate them into your style

Dave R. W. Graham

SUCCESS USUALLY COMES TO THOSE WHO ARE TOO BUSY TO BE LOOKING FOR IT.

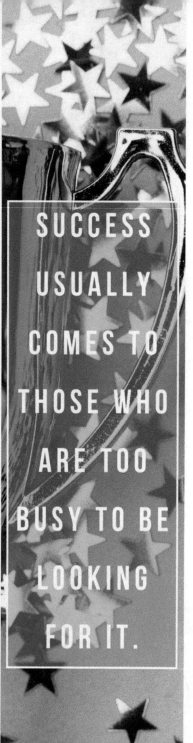

SUCCESS USUALLY COMES TO THOSE WHO ARE TOO BUSY TO BE LOOKING FOR IT.

Table of Content

Introduction

The stock market is the place investors associate with buy and sell investments, usually stocks, which are shares of proprietorship in an open organization. Stocks, otherwise called values, speak to fragmentary proprietorship in an organization, and the stock market is where investors can buy and sell responsibility for investible resources.

A stock market is considered monetary advancement as it enables companies to get capital from the general population rapidly. It is where shares of pubic recorded companies are exchanged. The essential market is the place companies glide shares to the overall population in the first sale of stock to raise capital.

Different elements go into the choices of traders and investors about where to buy and sell singular stocks. The most significant is the profitability of the organization, as well as its possibilities for profits. Traders are continually looking for advances.

They use past value activity as charts to illuminate their choices to sell or buy; however, whether they settle or not on the transaction depends on the events that will occur.

Most beginners—investors and traders—have quite confused ideas when approaching the stock market, investing in stocks (or options, ETFs, commodities, etc.) or trading in general. One of the pivotal points that creates confusion in those interested in making their money work through investments is the lack of understanding of the crucial difference between trading and investing.

The confusion derives from the fact that in the eyes of the investor or the uneducated and non-conscious trader, doing trading or investing seems to be the same thing.

Although they are united by the desire to make a profit, the two operations arise from different logic and follow different rules. Those who invest measure the value of what they buy (an action, a house, a business, an object of art, etc.), try to buy it at a discounted or otherwise balanced price.

The entire operation is based on the prediction or hope that, over time, the good purchased will increase in value and that this increase in value will automatically be reflected in a corresponding rise in its market price, allowing it to be sold for a profit.

An easily understandable example of investment is that of those who buy agricultural land in the expectation that it will then be buildable. The greatest investors of history, such as the legendary Warren Buffett, are, in fact, masters in buying "depreciated quality." Of course, their time horizon is never very short, and the value of what they have purchased can remain or even go down for a specified period without this causing them to worry excessively.

Trades, however, do not bet on a change in the value of things. The hard and pure trader does not care highly about the objective quality or the nature of what he buys and only interested in acquiring it at a price in a short time frame he plans to grow, even though the value of what he purchased remains perfectly identical.

What makes trading possible is that the prices of things and, therefore also investment objects such as shares, bonds, real estate, etc. may vary regardless of their value due to the law of supply and offer.

The stock market fills two significant needs. The first is to give money to companies that they can use to fund and grow their organizations. If an organization issues one million shares of stock that at the first sell for $10 an offer, at that point that furnishes the organization with $10 million of capital that it can use to develop its business less whatever expenses the organization pays for an investment bank to deal with the stock contribution.

By offering stock shares as opposed to getting the capital required for an extension, the organization abstains from bringing about obligation and paying interest charges on that obligation. The optional reason the stock market serves is to give investors, the individuals who buy stocks, a chance to partake in the profits of traded on an open market company.

The stock market empowers buyers and sellers to arrange costs and make exchanges. Investors would then be able to buy and sell these stocks among themselves, and the exchange tracks the organic market of each recorded stock.

It helps decide the cost for every security or the levels at which stock market members, investors, and traders are happy to buy or sell.

Chapter 1.

Factors Affecting the Stock Market

Topic Covered:

- Economy
- Political events
- Media
- Supply and Demand
- Natural Disasters
- Investors Themselves
- Marketing Hype

- World Events
- News
- Deflation
- When Should You Sell Your Stocks?
- Factors to Consider While Choosing A Stock

The stock market can be described by one unique element called change. It continues to change due to so many forces and influences. The volatility can be brought about by several issues. Take note that the following factors are not exhaustive. They are not the only factors that can affect the movement of stocks in the market, but have a role in the performance of stocks.

Economy

The economy is very much connected with the stock market. You can tell if the economy is doing well by looking at the stock market. States that have a good economy also tend to have a stable stock market.

Political events

As can be expected, the stock market cannot escape the influence of politics. For example, when JFK was assassinated, the U.S. stock market sank since investors were hesitant to invest. And, since stocks and bonds operate within a legal framework, the state's power to enact laws can also affect the stock market. After all, laws can directly affect many businesses.

Media

The media greatly affects the stock market. Due to the attention that the media can bring, it can either make or break companies, as well as their stocks. Media announcements can also cause lots of reactions, which can significantly affect the volatility of certain stocks.

Supply and Demand

As can be expected in any business, supply and demand affect the stock market. When the prices are low (high supply), many investors make a buy-in order, thereby creating demand. Then, the price will rise, and supply decreases. However, once the price gets too high, the demand drops, and the investors wait and look for other opportunities. Demand and supply will always fluctuate.

Occasionally, they may appear balanced. Part of their nature is a continuous fluctuation, which also affects the stock market.

Natural Disasters

As ironic as this may be, natural disasters tend to be beneficial to the stock market. This is because right after a natural disaster, people tend to spend lots of money on their rebuilding efforts and projects. Also, while natural disasters may damage the market for some time, they mostly initiate growth.

Investors Themselves

Each moment an investor purchases stock or makes a sell that affects the stock market. Now, just imagine how many investors engage in the same activity. For example, certain investors have confidence in a stock, and they purchase the said stock, and its price naturally increases. Say, due to the increased value, it manages to draw attention, and other people also start buying the same stocks. Now, when it has reached its peak, and the confidence in the stock begins to wane, the market simply collapses and fails.

Marketing Hype

It is so easy to promote something these days. You can easily share something with the world with just a few clicks of a mouse. Hence, many people have taken advantage of this by marketing some stocks to rise their value. In the stock market, the more attention the stocks draw, the higher their prices tend to increase. These days, some people promote themselves to be an "expert."

World Events

World events, regardless of whether good or bad, affect the stock market. They simply draw so much attention, and issues like having a change of leadership, international relations, and others, can either cause a boost in the market or cause it to panic.

News

News, especially that relating to businesses and the economy, can dramatically affect the stock market. Depending on the news, it can cause the value of stocks to rise or fall. Company news and announcements can also affect how investors analyze the market. If there is a likelihood of a company being successful, there will be an improvement in the performance of its stock and thus experience growth.

Deflation

When prices decrease, companies also experience lower profits, which also creates less economic activity. The prices of stocks may then drop, which will compel investors to share their shares and simply move to a more secure investment like bonds. These are some factors influencing a stock's volatility. It is suggested that you learn to understand just how these forces influence the performance of certain stocks, as well as market behavior.

When Should You Sell Your Stocks?

An important element in making money with stocks is to know when to sell them. Many investors lose their money not only because of choosing the wrong stocks to invest in. Sometimes, they lose their money by holding on for so long to what once was a good stock.

When the Company Shows Signs of Weakening

When a company experiences changes that are likely to weaken its performance, it is the right moment to sell the shares before it is too late. For example, when the sales of a company that has shown good performance through the years suddenly face a significant decline, it is time for you to reconsider whether it is still a good investment to keep your stocks in that company.

When the Company Removes Dividends

If there are no dividends at all or show signs of instability, it may indicate that the company is headed to no good. This is a serious red signal. When the situation occurs, you are advised to sell your stocks immediately.

When You Attain Your Objective

Many times, you can avoid losing your money by not being greedy. Some investors decide to sell their stocks once they are already satisfied with their profit. For example, say you buy certain stocks at $10 per share, and you aim to get a 50% profit. If the value of those stocks increases and reaches $15 (50% increase), you sell them right away. Avoid greediness and hope for it to reach $20 or even $16. By doing so, you get to minimize your risks, which also minimizes your losses.

Factors to Consider While Choosing a Stock

You must take the time to perform an analysis to select the right stocks to invest in. A wrong choice of stock can make you lose a lot of money and be a wastage of your precious time. Get more information about a given company you have an interest in and scrutinize their financial reports to know if you can invest with them. It is best to understand all the financial information you get about a company before making the final investment decision.

It is important to choose to invest in a business that is doing well. You will be able to enjoy the peace of mind that your investment will not waste and that you will enjoy the gains. To know if a company is performing well, be keen on some clues that include:

- The company's profit margin.

- A company's return on equity.

- Past performance and expected growth.

- Its historic rate of earnings growth compared to its peers.

- The debts that the company has.

- The debt-to-equity ratio, which means taking the company's debt and dividing it by shareholder equity. The lower the percentage is, the better and safer your investment will be.

Here are some factors that will help you make the right choice of stock to invest in:

Effective management of the business – It is a pertinent issue to study. However, not many investors can access how effective business management is; therefore, they do not consider this. Return on equity and the income shareholders earn per their investments is a great indication of how the business management uses the money investors have invested in the business. A business with a return on equity of 5% or more is a good one to consider investing in.

Stocks from a suitable business sector – It is important to choose the industry sectors where you want to invest it wisely. Some sectors do better than the others, which is why this is important. Do not concentrate on one sector of the economy; this can be risky for your investment. When you are diversifying, only go for stocks in the leading industry sectors to ensure that at least all stocks will perform well.

If, after some time, you will want to invest more money, you will invest in the sector that is doing better than the others. If there is a sector that is not doing well and you have already invested in it, you can always withdraw your investment as soon as possible and reinvest the money in a better performing sector.

The growing profits – Consider investing with a firm showing the potential for profits. Go for a company whose earnings per share growth is steady and at least 5% or more. This is what will assure you that you will be getting some money at the end of every year for as long as you will be investing in that company. Small companies are riskier to invest in the size of the company when compared to the big companies.

Big companies that have established themselves already know how to survive in the market; therefore, it is hard for such companies to go down. That is why they are the best to invest in. If possible, avoid penny stocks unless if you are willing to deal with all the risks involved. To be guaranteed of regular returns, buy stocks of big businesses.

Manageable debt – A business can borrow money to build itself, but too much debt is not good for the business. Ensure you have information on this before investing your money so that you will know if the debt per capita ratio is healthy or not. A rate of 0.5 or less is a good one, but if it is more, then there will be a problem after that. A business that is in debt will not be able to compensate its investors, and you might end up losing all your investment in the repayment of those debts.

Dividend payments – Companies that return part of their profits to the investors in terms of dividends are good companies to invest in. A dividend payment of 2% or more is a good one to consider and an important factor too. Dividends are important to investors. This is where the return on your investment on an annual basis comes in.

Stocks with enough liquidity are stocks that can easily be sold out if you no longer want to continue owning them. Some stocks are hard to sell, and these will give you a lot of problems when you finally want to sell them off. It is good to consider investing in stocks that will allow you to sell your position as fast as you want when the need arises.

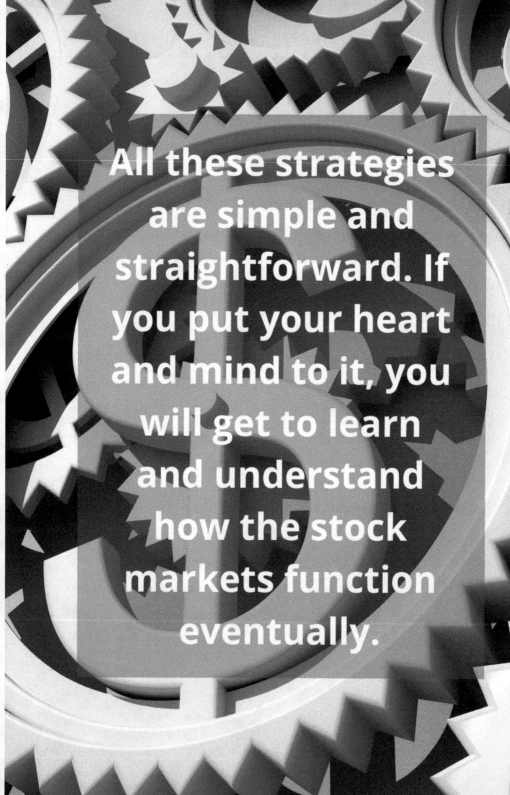

All these strategies are simple and straightforward. If you put your heart and mind to it, you will get to learn and understand how the stock markets function eventually.

Chapter 2.

Major Stock Exchanges

Topic Covered:

♦ The Four Major Exchanges

♦ Other Popular and Major Exchanges

♦ Stock Market Performance and Indexes

The stock market has a few major stock exchanges that are worth talking about in more detail. These markets are where most of the volume and liquidity (money) will be, thus the markets that have the most movement and profit to offer.

The Four Major Exchanges

NYSE

The New York Stock Exchange sees about $13.4 trillion in movement a day. The NYSE is the largest stock exchange in the world in terms of trade volume. It is also located in a physical location like all stock exchanges. The NYSE regulates stocks, commodities, and other product exchanges. Companies from around the world list their IPOs on the NYSE to gain the attention of investors.

Companies can be locally listed on their country's exchange and then launch on the NYSE when they become large enough to sustain the interest in their shares. Companies can only be listed on one exchange at a time to avoid regulatory issues, and some countries do not allow their companies to list on the NYSE. Any stock listed on the NYSE can be purchased by traders to make a profit and earn dividends.

In North America, there is more than one exchange, like the Philadelphia exchange and Toronto. However, it is the NYSE, Dow index, and NASDAQ that gets the most media.

Tokyo Stock Exchange

Japan's stock exchange is the TSE, and it sees $3.8 trillion in movement per day, although in 2014, it was listed as $4 trillion. The Tosho (TSE) is considered the third largest in terms of market cap, but the number of companies listed is only 2,292 making it the fourth largest for the number of companies listed on the exchange. In 2012, the TSE merged with Osaka Securities Exchange to become the JPX or Japan Exchange Group.

The exchange runs from 9 am to 11:30 am and from 12:30 to 3 pm during the weekdays. These are hours based on the Asian time zone.

LSE

The London Stock Exchange dealt with approximately $3.6 trillion market movement for the day before 2014. The LSE was formed in 1801 and, as of 2014, had $6.06 trillion as a market cap. The London Stock Exchange is considered the second largest by market cap data; however, it is behind the NASDAQ in terms of overall size. The LSE has merged with certain exchanges like Borsa Italiana, MTS, Turquoise, NASDAQ Bids, and there is a proposed merger with TMX Group.

The LSE has primary markets with premium listed main market companies, which are the biggest UK markets. There is the Alternative Investment Market for smaller companies, a professional securities market, and a specialist fund market. The LSE is open daily, on weekdays from 8 am to 4:30 pm, GMT.

Euronext

This is the European Stock Exchange. It was smaller, dealing with only $2.9 trillion in market movement per day before the split with the NYSE. In 2015, the exchange started seeing closer to $3.7 trillion as a market cap. This was after Euronext made a public offering to become a separate entity.

The market offers equities, exchange-traded funds, bonds, derivatives, commodities, warrants and certificates, and indices. It was established as an exchange in Amsterdam, London, Brussels, Paris, and Lisbon, as well as part of the Intercontinental Exchange.

Other Popular and Major Exchanges

In this list, you will see three other major exchanges, which are popular in certain markets like Asian stock investments. They are listed because they have a higher market cap in comparison to other exchanges that exist around the world:

Shanghai Stock Exchange
Shanghai is another Asian market that sees a high volume of $2.7 trillion.

Hong Kong Stock Exchange
Hong Kong has the same amount of traffic as the Shanghai Market.

Toronto Stock Exchange
Toronto is home to Canada's stock exchange. The market cap for this exchange is $2.2 trillion.

Stock Market Performance and Indexes

The NASDAQ and Dow Jones are two important indexes to discuss and determine market performance. Each needs to be explained to help you understand how the stock market works.

NASDAQ
The NASDAQ is a stock exchange that also offers options trading. It is an exchange that was the first electronic stock market, which lowered the spread charged to investors. The spread is the difference between the buy and sell price and is where most brokerage firms make their money.

The NASDAQ offers a premarket period to fit into the London Stock Exchange part of the trading system. These hours are 4 am to 9:30 am EST and then from 9:30 am to 4 pm for the normal trading session. There is a post-market session that fits in the Asian time zone trading period, and those hours are 4 pm to 8 pm.

The NASDAQ has market tiers: small, mid, and large-cap. They are referred to as the capital, global, and global select market, respectively.

The stock exchange sees $9.6 trillion in daily movement. Approximately 3,600 companies are listed on the exchange. Investors can do more on the NASDAQ with options trading than on other exchanges. Options are a complicated process that you will want advanced stock market investing information to understand. You need to know it is an exchange with a different list of companies than the NYSE that may offer you room to grow into options trading.

The Dow Jones

It is a stock market index that measures the price of a specific unit of the stock market. It is computed based on selected stocks based on an average of the price of these shares. Investors use it to figure out the market movement and market health based on the average prices of top companies.

Mutual funds and exchange-traded funds tend to use this type of index to track what the funds will do or have done in reacting to news and economic data. The Dow Jones was the first stock market index to be started. It was devised by Charles Dow in 1896. Edward Jones was his partner and a statistician. They weight 30 components that have to do with traditional industries.

Stock market investors will use the Dow Jones to determine the performance of a specific industry sector for American companies and overall weighting of the USA's economic stability. The Dow Jones is not meant to be influenced by economic reports or corporate reports, but by price movement alone.

You can use the Dow Jones for ETF, leverage, short funds, futures contracts and options contracts. When you hear media experts talking about the market going up or down by a certain number of "points," they are usually talking about the Dow Jones index computation.

Chapter 3.

Indexing

Topic Covered:

- The Basic Guidelines of an Indexing Strategy
- How to Pick Stocks for an Index Portfolio
- Where Will You Buy?
- Available funds
- Reasonable costs
- Pick Your Index
- Capitalization and Size
- Sector or Industry
- Geography
- Market Opportunities
- Type of Asset

Indexing is a passive investment style that buys index-tracking funds in various markets. Rather than buying individual stocks, you buy an entire market. It's a convenient way to diversify without too much effort or concern about picking the right stocks. We'll go over the basics of how an indexing strategy works and how you choose index funds or ETFs to include in your portfolio.

The Basic Guidelines of an Indexing Strategy

An index is a collection of stocks that have all been grouped according to some common factors and criteria. Then, they invest in this collection of stocks, spreading the actual investments across each stock according to their price relative to the rest of the group.

The most well-known indices are the ones that track entire markets like the Dow or the S&P. These index funds invest in the entirety of those markets and are said to be "tracking the market." As a result, you don't have to worry about the individual performance of any one stock in the market. Instead, your returns will be whatever the Dow's or the S&P's overall returns are.

Market indices aren't the only ones out there, though. Index funds can be created around any idea or characteristic. There are index funds that track specific industries like healthcare or energy.

There are a few advantages to index funds. The main advantage is that it's an incredibly easy way to diversify your portfolio. Rather than meticulously researching thousands of stocks for the ones you want to invest in, you can pick an index fund (or a few index funds) that agrees with your investing style and then invest in those. Your money is automatically diversified across the entire group of stocks the index is tracking.

This makes them extremely convenient and easy to use. Even the most novice investor can use index investing as an easier way to diversify and minimize risk while still enjoying a healthy return.

It can also be a lot more affordable since it's a more passive form of investing. The less active management a fund requires, the less fees investors must pay. When you invest in index funds, you're generally using a buy-and-hold strategy that will require little active trading over time, so you won't be paying as much in transaction fees, taxes, or other expenses that go along with investing.

As your wealth grows, however, an index fund becomes a less attractive choice. Even the most passive index fund is still being managed by someone, meaning you're earning a little less per share than you would if you had privately invested in the same set of stocks, using the same proportions.

This slight difference is not worth considering for the average investor because, in general, the average investor doesn't have the capital needed to perfectly recreate an index portfolio, complete with the same weighting of stocks. In other words, most investors can't afford to buy full shares of every stock in an index.

When you invest in an index fund, however, you don't need to worry about that. The fund managers will spread the money you do have evenly across all their stocks, even if that ends up spreading so that you aren't buying a full share in every stock.

When your money has grown, however, an index investor would benefit from shifting away from index funds and towards building their index portfolio. Then, you could keep your money diversified in the same way that it has been up to this point, but you'll be pocketing even more of the returns by paying less in fees.

How to Pick Stocks for an Index Portfolio

Not all index funds are created equal. Within the index's world, you can still choose between more active investing styles and more passive ones. Before investing in any index fund, you do want to do your research to investigate the important details like:

- The past performance of the index fund itself.

- Any news and information that would be relevant to the stocks included in the fund. For example, for an energy index fund, you want to do your research about the energy industry and what kinds of policies, global trade news, natural disasters, technological developments, and others could influence the performance of the stocks in that index.

Where Will You Buy?

You've already read about the differences between ETFs and mutual funds. It's the difference between directly investing your money into the index fund or trading shares of it on the open market. If you don't plan on doing much active trading, direct investment in the mutual fund may be your best bet.

Once you've decided whether you're going to invest directly or buy ETFs, you need to choose your broker. When choosing a broker, consider the following factors:

Available funds

What kind of index funds does that broker offer? How do they perform against similar index funds from their competitors? If you're going the ETF route, you need to make sure the broker offers ETF trading.

Additional services

Ideally, you want to find a single broker who can meet all your needs. If you're planning to put your money in and then just let it grow, you don't need too many additional services. However, if you're buying ETFs, you may want stock research, screening tools, portfolio management tools, or investing educational resources.

Reasonable costs

More and more brokers are offering free transactions (either unlimited or a fixed amount). However, mutual funds still charge commissions, and those prices increase; the more active management is required to maintain the fund.

Pick Your Index

An index funds track a variety of indices. This step is likely where the bulk of your research is going to happen as an index investor. While you are not limited to just picking one index, you still want to have in-depth knowledge of any index you choose. Here's a quick breakdown of the broad types of index funds you'll find:

Capitalization and Size

These are index funds that track stocks based on size. You can find large-cap indices, small-cap indices, or mid-cap indices. The large-cap index would be made up of larger, more stable stocks while the smaller ones would be less stable but potentially offer higher growth. So, you'll be making some of the same decisions that a value or growth investor would make, except for larger collections of stocks rather than individual stocks.

Sector or Industry

Another way to group stocks into an index is by sector or industry. You can find tech index funds, good consumer funds, and so on, all the stocks within that sector. Then, whatever the average returns are for that sector, that will be the returns on your index fund. With these types, you must be careful about the sector you pick. The up-and-down cycle of a single sector can be more dramatic than that of the market. So, you usually want to choose a few different sector index funds rather than putting everything into one.

Geography

Index funds defined by geography generally trade foreign markets. Rather than a Dow or S&P index, you might invest in an even broader index that tracks the entire US market.

Geographically defined indices are a great way to diversify your portfolio beyond your home market and to protect against recessions because a recession in the US doesn't necessarily mean every market in the world is in a recession.

You can hedge yourself against bear markets by investing in an index that's tracking another market altogether, ideally one that's more bullish than your own.

Market Opportunities

Market opportunity indices track growing sectors or emerging markets in search of stronger growth opportunities. They require a lot more research on your part because, by nature, they are a little riskier than other funds.

Type of Asset

The least popular type of index is one that tracks a particular asset class. For example, you can invest in a bond index fund that tracks government bonds from different countries around the world or a domestic bond fund that tracks federal, state, and corporate bonds within a single market.

Other assets that tend to get grouped into an index include cash and commodities like oil.

Chapter 4.

Price Action Strategies

Topic Covered:

♦ Make Use of Covered Calls

♦ Strike Price

♦ Expiration Date

You do not need to be hitting home runs to be successful in the stock market. You should focus on getting the base hits and try to grow your portfolio by taking the most gains in the range of 20%-25%. While it may sound counterintuitive, it is always best to sell a stock when it's on the rise, consistently advancing and looking appealing to all other investors. As you may have already figured out, trading on the stock market is a risky business, though the rewards that can come from these risks make it all worth it. Even though you will never be able to eliminate the risks, there are some things you can do to mitigate risks by actively managing your portfolio and making clever investments.

However, if you are not careful or don't know what you're doing, you could end up paying a pretty hefty price. The buy low and sell high strategy might have resulted in the success of many investors, but it is not how the real professionals become successful. Instead, smart investors deploy their money strategically to allow it to work in more ways than one. In layman's terms, they multitask their money. There are ways to maximize your profits and get the most out of your investments.

If you were to think of investing like a game, the way you would win would be to purchase a stock at a low price and then sell in the future at a higher price. If you are a homeowner, then you likely understand this concept quite practically. It's best to use one of two strategies to make a profit on your investment.

The first is value investing, Like the products you buy from stores every day, stocks go on sale now and then, and value investors wait for this sale to happen. This makes it easier for them to make a profit, since stocks that are undervalued, or on sale, have more room for growth.

Unfortunately, your favorite stock might not be suited to this strategy since it must pay a dividend. It would need to have a price low enough for you to buy 100 shares, and it needs to trade many shares every day - at least 1 million shares of the daily volume are preferable.

You also want to avoid highly volatile stocks, as their more unpredictable shifts in price are more difficult to manage. This is where your stock evaluation skills and research will be put to the test.

Once you have found your stock, and you have decided that you want to value invest, you want this name to be in the middle or near the bottom of the trading range for the last 52 weeks. If it is not currently there, then you should either find another company or wait for the stock to be at a price you are willing to pay for.

The second strategy is known as momentum trading. Some investors believe that the best time for a stock to be bought is when its price continues to rise, since, as we learned in school, objects in motion tend to remain in motion. Most people want to think of the long term, as the longer you have stock, the better its potential returns can be.

Make Use of Covered Calls

Covered calls are slightly more complex. Using the method of purchasing a stock and collecting its dividend as it increases will still provide you with some significant gains. There are two important questions before you sell a covered call:

- What is the strike price?

- How many months do you want your contract to last for?

Strike Price

Covered calls are a kind of options contract strategy that allows the contract holder to purchase your 100 shares if it is at the strike price or above it. You probably do not want someone to take your shares from you, so the strike price will need to be steep enough that the stock does not rise above it, but low enough that you can collect a decent premium for taking a risk.

This is a pretty tough decision to make, especially for new investors such as yourself. If your stock is currently experiencing a downtrend, you will likely be able to sell an option with a strike price not much higher than the current actual price of the stock.

However, if the stock is experiencing an uptrend, you may want to wait until you are happy that the move up has run its course and that the stock will soon shift in the opposite direction. Remember that whenever a stock appreciates, your option value depreciates.

Expiration Date

The further you take your option into the future, the bigger your premium payout will be upfront, to sell the call, but that also means more time that your stock needs to be below the strike price, to avoid it being 'called away' from you. Consider going three or four months ahead for your first contract.

As soon as you sell it, your covered call will make money for you, since the premium paid by the buyer will be deposited into your account directly. It will keep making money for you even if your stock's price drops. The premium falls with the price. You can buy back the contract from the buyer at any time, so, if the premium does fall, you can buy it for less than what you sold it for.

That means you're making a profit. At the same time, if your stock were to rise above the strike price, you would be able to buy the contract for more than you sold it, causing a loss, but also saving you need to hand over 100 of your shares. One of the most effective ways to use the covered call is to collect the premium at the beginning.

Even though you can repurchase the option if its price shifts, you will want to only do so under dire circumstances. It would be best if you kept in mind that the money you collect from selling your covered call can also be deducted from the price you paid for the stock.

The easiest way to get the hang of a new investment strategy is to make use of a virtual platform, like the ones many brokerage firms offer in their apps or websites. You can still buy the stock and collect dividends, but wait to sell the covered call until you feel comfortable with the way it works.

Chapter 5.

Classifications of Stock Market Investors

Topic Covered:

- ♦ The Conservative Investor
- ♦ Fundamental Trader
- ♦ Sentiment Trader
- ♦ The Intermediate Investor
- ♦ Market Timer
- ♦ Arbitrage Trader
- ♦ The Risk Taker
- ♦ Noise Trader

There is no doubt that stock investing provides a great opportunity to earn money. However, an investor must know when the best time is to buy or sell stocks. Before you begin investing in stocks, you may want to know first what type of investor you are.

The Conservative Investor

A conservative investor is an individual who does not take capital growth as an utmost priority when investing. Instead, he seeks for stable investments that can flourish gradually and practically not susceptible to high volatility. A conservative investor usually obtains moderate capital growth and a steady income stream.

They may not get much from their investments, but they make sure to get a steady flow of earnings regularly. The conservative investor is cautious in making investment decisions.

Fundamental Trader

A fundamental trader is someone who focuses on company-specific affairs to help determine the right stock to buy and the best time to buy it. To depict this in another way, suppose this type of trader has decided to visit a shopping mall.

A fundamental trader is someone who makes decisions based on fundamental things. They will visit each store, study the products that each store offers, and then arrive at the final decision of either making a purchase or not. The same thing happens when it comes to buying stocks. They may study them first before he/she decides to make a purchase.

Trading on fundamentals can be a short-term or a long-term endeavor. It is often associated more with the investing strategy known as buy and hold than short-term trading. Some trading strategies rely on split-second decisions, and others depend on factors or trends that play out within the day. The fundamentals may remain the same for months or years.

The quarterly release of the target company's financial statement can provide valuable information regarding the firm's financial health or position in the stock market. Changes or lack of it can give a trader a sort of signal whether to trade or not. A press release that brings bad news has the power to overturn everything in an instant.

Many investors find fundamental trading appealing because it is based on facts and logic—It practically ensures no room for errors. However, finding and deciphering the facts may take time, and it is a research-intensive task.

Sentiment Trader

A sentiment trader does not try to outsmart the market by seeking securities that may bring huge earnings. Instead, he identifies the securities that move with the market's momentum.

Most sentiment traders combine technical and fundamental analysis features to help them identify and take part in the market movements.

There are sentiment traders that aim to seize momentous movements in price and try to keep away from idle times. Some traders try to take advantage of indicators of excessive negative or positive sentiment that may provide a sign of a possible reversal in sentiment.

The key challenges that sentiment traders usually face:

- Market volatility
- Trading costs
- Difficulty in making accurate predictions regarding market sentiment

If you think you are a conservative investor, your success depends on your ability to decipher the stocks that can give a steady flow of income. You may not get large amounts of money, but you will always gain something with little to no risk involved.

The Intermediate Investor

The intermediate investor takes some risks but still makes certain that the initial capital he invests will remain secure. This type of investor usually owns a rather volatile portfolio. These investors expect good (or near exceptional) capital growth.

They may face some market fluctuations, which is unlikely to happen under normal market conditions. They usually own a balanced portfolio with assets that include a combination of bonds and stocks from established companies with a good record. This trader may choose to make a small investment in riskier assets that can provide better capital growth.

Market Timer

A market timer is a trader who tries to guess whether security will move up or down and if such a move can generate profit. To guess the direction of the movement, this trader checks the economic data or technical indicators. Some investors strongly believe that the direction of market movement is impossible to predict.

Market timers with long-term track records won't deny that it is quite challenging to achieve success using this method. Most investors know that they need to dedicate more time to gain a reliable level of success. These investors believe that long-term strategies are lucrative and, therefore, more rewarding.

Arbitrage Trader

This trader usually purchases and sells assets simultaneously to gain a substantial profit from price differences of financial instruments that are related or identical.

Arbitrage traders buy particular security in one market and sell it simultaneously at a higher price in a different market, taking advantage of the price difference. It is considered a riskless trade that can provide pure profit to the investor.

Let us use foreign exchange in our example to illustrate. A trader buys stock from a foreign exchange that is yet to adjust the price for the fluctuating exchange rate. At that time, the price of the foreign exchange is undervalued when you compare it against the local exchange. The trader can take advantage of it and generate profit from the price disparity.

Arbitrage exists due to market inefficiencies. It provides a means to keep prices from deviating too much from fair value for a long time. Understand that all markets can't impose uniform prices at the same time. Security may be traded at a lower price in one exchange market and a higher price in another market.

An arbitrage trader may still gain a lot of profit now, but one should not underestimate the technology advancement. Soon, it may become difficult to gain profit from a price disparity.

The intermediate investors may look like conservative investors at times, but they are not afraid to take some risks from time to time. Be extra careful when trading with risky stocks. You may gain more advantage than a conservative investor when you do that.

The Risk Taker

The risk-takers are dynamic investors willing to trade with greater risk to maximize profits. The investment portfolio of such trader could include stocks of young or new companies and emerging market equities. It may also contain a higher percentage of stock than bonds.

Noise Trader

In noise trading, whenever a trader buys or sells something, he does not refer to the fundamental data specific to a company that issues the securities. Noise traders commonly engage in short-term trades to gain profit from different economic trends.

Noise traders overreact to any good or bad news surrounding the stock market, and they have poor timing. The technical analysis of statistics that the market activity has generated could turn into useless data. They can't properly investigate the volume and past prices of the market that can somehow help them gain some insights on market activity and direction in the future.

Let us go back to the example that we had about the shopping mall. As compared to a fundamental analyst, a technical analyst may only sit outside and collect data regarding the number of people that each store has. He does not care about the products sold in each store. It is enough that he could see the number of people that each store can attract to help him arrive at a certain decision.

Most people can be considered as noise traders. Only some individuals use fundamental analysis when deciding on the investment.

If you are willing to trade stocks without knowing or weighing possible consequences that such trade may yield, you are a risk-taker. You may be able to earn much profit at once and then lose some at other times if you are too reckless.

So, what type of investor are you? You may need to improve something to make sure that you will gain more profits. Knowing the characteristics or psyche of a good investor can help you a lot.

Chapter 6.

Active and Passive Stock Investing

Topic Covered:

♦ Active Investing

♦ Passive Investing

♦ Active versus Passive Investments

When it comes to making money from stocks, there are two ways to do it: actively and passively. And it's by understanding the difference between the two that you'll have a better idea of what investing and trading mean.

Active Investing

As you could infer from the term itself, active investing means a relatively high degree of activity. In other words, you'll need to be more active or involved in managing your stock investments. This means that on top of doing your homework in terms of choosing your stocks wisely, you'll need to monitor its performance regularly, depending on your investment time frame, i.e., short or long term.

These are the things you'll need to do if you choose the active investing route:

Research and Evaluate: What makes investing in the stock market much different from gambling in a casino, which some "geniuses" think is a very apt comparison, is that you don't just pick random stocks to trade or invest in and expect success. No, you'll need to research and evaluate stocks based on the information you're able to gather to come up with a candidates' shortlist. And from such a shortlist, you'll pick the stocks in which to trade or invest.

Take Positions: All the research and evaluation in the world will be for naught if that's where you'll end your journey. You'll need to act based on the information you've gathered and evaluated by taking a position on any or all the stocks in your shortlist, i.e., buy stocks.

Unless you take actual positions, you will not earn anything from stocks. When you buy stocks, you're taking a LONG position. When you're selling stocks that you own, you're taking a SQUARE position. And when you sell shares of stocks that you do not own, you're taking a SHORT position.

Monitoring: When you're after a very quick buck with every stock purchase you make, the more important it is for you to keep track of the price of your stocks frequently. It's because there's a very good chance that you might miss the quick profits boat if you don't check market prices every few hours. And even if you're in it for the long haul, you will still need to monitor stock prices to make sure your investments are performing as desired, albeit less frequently say every week or every month.

At this point, I'd like to bring to your attention the words "trading" and "investment," in case you're wondering why I'm using them both or interchangeably. Here's the reason: Trading is the term often used to refer to very short investment periods.

When stock market veterans say they're "trading" stocks, what they're saying is that their investment horizons are very, very short. How short? The longest would probably be a couple of days to a week, while many trades are daily. After they buy, they wait for the price to go up several points within the day of the week, and they quickly sell their shares to cash in on the profits. People who "trade" stocks this way must do it frequently so that over a month or a year, their small profits accumulate into a much bigger total.

On the other hand, "investing" is often taken to mean as holding on to shares of stocks or any financial asset for a relatively long period. In many instances, investing is taken to mean as a minimum investment holding period of about three months and is often referred to as a "buy-and-hold" approach. Just buy stocks and leave it be.

However, there's no official barometer for considering whether a specific investment holding period is considered as trading or investing.

It's because when you look at the grand scheme of things, trading and investing are practically the same and the only difference, albeit an arbitrary one, is the time frame.

The goal of trading is buying-and-holding, which is to earn a profit. And either way, that's what investing is! And when you talk about the primary way you will successfully earn money via stock market investing, which is capital appreciation, it involves buying stocks at a low price and selling them at a higher one. And that's the real definition of trading, i.e., buying and selling.

Passive Investing

Passive investments are very popular these days, sometimes for the right reasons, but mostly for the wrong ones. For one, many personal finances "gurus" have painted passive investing to be the financial savior of every individual on earth who's living in poverty today.

For others, many such gurus also make it appear—albeit not purposefully—as if building passive income streams that generate enough passive income is easy. And lastly, the same so-called gurus make it appear that passive investing is passive, i.e., a perfectly inactive form of investing where you do nothing, and riches will continue flowing to you. But is passive investing all that? Let's find out, shall we?

Passive investing is taken from the word "passive," which means, among other things, inactive. Therefore, many people have the impression that passive investing means practically waiting for money just to come in. Now, this is where I'll have to shed a bit lighter on passive investing.

Passive investing means very little work or effort is needed to generate money. By inactive, what we're trying to say here is much less work. There's no such thing as a free—or inactive—lunch. You will always have to do something, even if it's very little.

The general passive investing approach taken by many is the buy-and-hold approach to make money in the stock market.

Compared to the active trading approach where you must monitor the market prices of your stocks very frequently and transact much more frequently, passively investing in stocks allows you to do other things during the day like work on a day job or enjoy life.

Profit does not come from a particular winning investment, but from a series of winning and losing investments

It's also way less stressful. But still, it's not a completely inactive activity. And you can earn much more via trading. So, there's your tradeoff: less work, fewer earnings vs. more work, more earnings.

Another reality about passive investing, you'll need to be aware of is that earning a significant enough amount of income to live on and become rich from is neither easy nor cheap! What do I mean by this?

Let's say your goal is to live off passive income from stocks and that your average annual living expenses amount to $36,000. If the average annual rate of return on stock investments is 10%, you'll need to have at least $360,000 passively invested in stocks to make $36,000 annually.

If you're in dire financial straits, it means you really can't rely on passive income to get you out of poverty or your current state of need. The only passive source of income that can do that for you is winning the lottery.

Active versus Passive Investments

Now that you're aware of what active and passive stock market investing looks like, which do you think will be more advantageous to you? Right off the bat, there's no outright winner because each approach has its advantages and disadvantages. What will determine the best approach for you will be your goals and current personal circumstances.

For example, if you don't have much time to spare to monitor your stock market investments on an hourly or bi-hour basis because of your day job, then passive stock market investing's the appropriate one for you. It's also the more appropriate type of stock market investing for you if you want to keep things simple and uncomplicated, and if your risk tolerance is relatively low.

But if you're the type who has all the time to do practically nothing else but watch the stock market throughout the day, and have a high tolerance, then active stock trading may be the better approach for you.

But what about in terms of profitability? Which of the two are generally more profitable? I'll give this round to active trading.

Why? It's because it's highly unlikely to make money in stocks when the markets are down. Not impossible but highly unlikely. But with active trading, you can still make money even when the markets are crashing down.

Keep in mind that I'm not saying passive investing isn't profitable, only that per my experience, an active trading approach to stock market investing's normally the more lucrative or profitable one.

Chapter 7.

Tips and Tricks

Topic Covered:

- Growth at Reasonable Price (GARP) Investing:
- Growth Investing
- Value Investing
- Buy and Hold
- Price Action Trading

Growth at Reasonable Price (GARP) Investing:

The GARP method of investing is a combination of both growth and value investing. It looks for companies that are currently slightly undervalued and have sustainable growth potential. It typically looks for stocks that are currently somewhat less undervalued than those that value investing; while expecting slightly less from the stocks it chooses than growth investing. Much like growth investing, GARP investing is concerned with the growth of a prospective company. When using this method, see positive earnings from the past few years as well as positive earnings projections for the coming years. Unlike with growth investing, however, the ideal range of growth in the next five years is going to be between 25 and 50 percent instead of 100 percent.

The theory here is that higher growth rates lead to high rates of risk. GARP investing is also going to share metrics for potential companies with growth investing, though the ideal levels are going to be lower. A good company to invest in with the GARP method sees positive cash flow and positive earnings momentum. Outside of that, however, you are going to have some more freedom when it comes to choosing the best companies when using this strategy, as subjectivity is an inherent part of GARP investing.

Regardless of the specifics, it is important to always analyze companies in relation to their unique contexts, as there is no ideal formula for what makes a good GARP investment.

Growth Investing

Whereas value investors are the most concerned with where a company is currently, growth investors are more focused on the potential future growth of a company to the point of barely considering the current price at all. This investment strategy focuses on buying into companies that are currently trading above their intrinsic value with the belief that this intrinsic value will continue to grow to the point that it exceeds current valuations.

To utilize this strategy effectively, first keep an eye on young companies, as they are traditionally going to grow more rapidly than more established companies.

The theory behind this strategy success is that this growth in revenue or earnings will then directly translate to an increase in the underlying stock price. Other common investments include companies in rapidly expanding industries, frequently those that are related to new technologies. Profits are then realized not through dividends but through capital gains, as it is uncommon for growth companies to pay dividends as they typically reinvest the money that would be going to dividends directly back into the company instead.

Unlike most of the other strategies, there are no hard and fast guidelines when it comes to investing in growth companies. However, there are certain criteria which can be used as a framework for your analysis; these must be applied to each company with an eye towards a company's unique situation.

Some of the things you will want to keep in mind include the company's current state as compared to past performance and its performance compared to its industry as a whole.

Value Investing

This investment strategy is exceedingly simple to understand, though it can be difficult to execute in practice. To successfully value invest, all you need to do is seek out companies that are currently trading below their current worth.

To do so, you will want to start by looking for stocks that feature quality fundamentals including cash flow, book value, dividends, and earnings. When you find a company that is currently undervalued based on these fundamentals, pounce to take full advantage before the market corrects itself.

You need to understand that the key here is to look for value, not junk. This is a crucial difference, otherwise, you will simply find yourself holding on to a stock whose company continues to decline in value.

One of the biggest proponents of this type of investing is Warren Buffet. He held the stock for his holding company Berkshire Hathaway starting in 1967 when it was worth $12 per share and by 2002 it was worth $70,900 per share. While these results are far from average, it goes to show how potentially profitable this type of strategy can be if pursued correctly.

If you intend to venture into value investing, you need to ensure that the share price is not greater than two-thirds of stock's value. Additionally, you are going to want to look for companies that have a P/E ratio in the bottom 10 percent of all equity securities. The price/earnings to growth ratio, which is the P/E ratio divided by the growth rate of the company's earnings, should be less than one.

Furthermore, the stock price should never be more than the tangible book value, and the company should have less debt than it does equity.

The company's current assets should be at least twice that of its current liabilities, and its dividend yield should be a minimum of two-thirds of its long-term bond yield. Its earnings growth should be a minimum of 7 percent per annum when compounded for the last 10 years.

Finally, it is important to always factor in a margin of safety as well. A margin of safety is simply a little wiggle room when it comes to potential errors that may have occurred when you were calculating the intrinsic value of the company. To add in a margin of error, all you need to do is subtract 10 percent from the intrinsic value number.

Buy and Hold

The buy and hold strategy is a type of passive investment in which, as the name implies, shareholders buy into a stock that has strong long-term potential and then hold onto it even when the markets see a downturn.

This strategy looks to the efficient market to be a hypothesis for success, which states that it is impossible to see above-average returns when adjusting for risk. This means that it is never a good idea to resort to active trading. It also says that seeing decreases in value in the short term is fine as long as the long-term trend remains positive.

The strategy is effective in minimizing the commissions and fees that you have to pay a brokerage because you will only have to do so once before generating an eventual profit. In this strategy, you also don't have to worry about timing the market which is useful for new investors as determining when to buy low and sell high can be much more difficult than it first appears.

For the effectiveness of the strategy, you need to start at an early age. If an investor first bought stocks in 1960 and held onto them for 50 years, then they would have seen nearly a 40 percent return on their investment, while someone who bought in starting in 2000 would have since seen a loss of little more than 2 percent if they sold today. It is easy to get started with this strategy.

All you need to do is research where several companies are currently and consider their future projections to ensure they seem to be moving in the right direction.

Once the stock is purchased, all you need to do is to check in on your investments from time to time and ensure that nothing catastrophic has happened. Additionally, adopting this strategy means that you will have to pay less in income taxes; specifically, capital gains are taxed at a much lower rate in the long-term than they are in the short-term.

The disadvantages of this type of strategy include the possibility for nearly unlimited losses because you are not checking on the stock that frequently, nor are you watching the markets on a regular basis; you could easily stumble into a situation where the stock in question dropped far enough that it is unlikely that you would ever be able to see enough positive gains again to properly right the ship. Additionally, get to understand the difference between irretrievable losses and expected decreases. So, if you panic and make a move when it is not required, then you will be stuck with a loss that could have eventually been mitigated when the market righted itself.

Price Action Trading

At its most fundamental, price action trading can be thought of as a way for a trader to determine the current state of the market based on what it currently looks like, what any number of indicators says about it after the fact. This is a great strategy for those who are interested in getting started as quickly as possible, as you are only required to study the market in its current form.

Additionally, focusing on just the price will make it easier to avoid much of the largely superfluous information that is circling the market causing static, which makes it more difficult to determine what is really going on.

In order to determine when to trade using price action, you will need to use the trading platform that came with the brokerage you chose and utilize what is known as price bars, which are a representation of price information over a specific period of time, broken down into weekly, daily, 1 hour, 30-minute or 5-minute intervals

To create an accurate price bar, you need the open price for the given stock in the chosen time frame, the high for the time frame, the low for the time frame, and the closing price. With this data, you should end up with a box with a line through it. The line represents the high and the low for the day while the edges of the box show the opening and closing prices.

In addition to summarizing the information for the timeframe in question, it also provides relevant information for your purposes. This includes the range of the stock, which is a representation of how volatile the market currently is. The bigger the box in relation to the line, the more active and volatile the market currently is. The more volatile the market currently is, the more risk you undertake when making a move.

In addition to the range, consider the physical orientation of the box; if the close price is above the open price, then the market improved over the timeframe; if the close is below the open, then the market lost value.

Take into account the size of the box as a whole. The bigger the box, the stronger the market is overall. What this type of strategy provides you with is a clear idea of what the levels of resistance and support are like for the observed time frame.

This, in turn, allows you to pick trades with a higher degree of certainty. All you need to do is keep in mind that if demand is stronger than supply, the price is going to increase and vice versa.

If the movement indicates that this is likely to continue in the same direction, then you will want to pick the point where it is likely to happen again and use that as your entry point. If the opposite is true, then you are going to want to sell ASAP to prevent yourself from losing out on gains you have already seen.

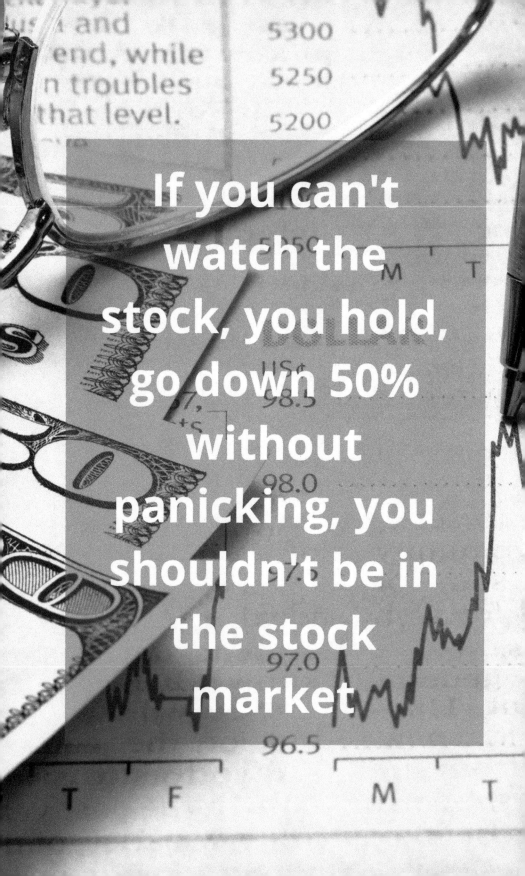

If you can't watch the stock, you hold, go down 50% without panicking, you shouldn't be in the stock market

Chapter 8.

Stock Orders

Topic Covered:

♦ Market and Limit Orders

♦ All or None Orders

♦ Stop Order and Stop Limit Orders

♦ Buy to Cover and Sell Short Orders

♦ Trailing Stop Orders

♦ Bracketed Orders

♦ Day Orders, GTC Orders, and Extended Hours Orders

There are types of stock orders that you can make. All of these can be accomplished by calling your broker with the instructions to execute the trade.

Market Orders

This is the utmost common kind of trading stocks. When you place a market order, you take the price presented to you when the order is executed. For instance, if you are interested in buying stocks from Microsoft and the price per stock is $90.23, you may end up getting it for $89.48 or $92.46. Therefore, the commission you pay your broker varies as well.

Limit Orders

You set a predetermined amount (the limit) that you are willing to buy or sell the stocks. First, your limit order may never be executed. Why? It is because the chance that share prices will rise or fall to your intended amount is next to none. Second, brokers execute limit orders based on the order they are received. This means that you might be looking at an excellent chance of your limit order being executed at the time you sent it. when your broker comes across it on the "queue," price for the stock you are eyeing may have already increased or decreased beyond your limit

All or None Orders

In normal circumstances, a bulk order for common stocks requires that the order be filled by your broker when the opportunity arises. This means that a single bulk order may be completed within weeks. This mechanism is in place to prevent sudden shifts in the market brought about by bulk stock purchases or sales. There are moments you may need to purchase stocks in bulk. It may be that the current share price for that company is within your budget. It may also be that you wanted to become a shareholder for that company. Regardless of your plans, it is possible to accomplish bulk orders of stocks in a single transaction through all-or-none trading. This order tells your broker that unless he or she can execute the order in one transaction, your order will remain outstanding.

Stop Order and Stop Limit Orders

These trading types are what people have been talking about if you have heard of' stop-loss. 'The purpose of this is obvious: To avoid losses and lock in profits resulting from a profitable trade. Let's discuss each of them.

Stop orders are executed once a stop price is reached. A stop price is a predetermined amount that triggers the execution of the order. In other words, once the stop price materializes, stop orders automatically become market orders. Stop orders are guaranteed to be executed. You will not know the actual share price until it is executed.

Stop limit orders, on the other hand, converts to a limit order when the stop price is reached. Still, in conjunction with share price, the order may or may not be executed.

Buy to Cover and Sell Short Orders

Both trading types are highly speculative and can lead to unlimited losses. However, if your speculations turn out to be correct, you can stand to make a profit. Note that to sell short and buy to cover orders, you must hold the belief that the current share price is overvalued and that the price will decrease to its actual value in the future. So, what you can do here is to place a short sell order for 100 shares. Multiply it by the current share price of $100, and you get $1,000. Now, you approach your broker to borrow $1,000 worth of Twitter shares to cover for your short sell. You go to the open market and sell the shares. As you make a sale, you pocket the cash.

If in the future, your speculated share price for Twitter will become $50, you will repurchase the 100 shares you have sold for $50 through a buy-to-cover order. The amount of the buy to cover the order will now be $500. So, you can now return the shares you borrowed from your broker and keep the $500 profit. To successfully carry out short sell and buy to cover orders, you need two things:

- That your brokerage account is a margin account. Meaning that the account allows you to borrow money from your broker.

- That your money in the account is enough to pay your broker back if the shares you are keeping an eye on actual increase in the price instead of decreasing as you expected.

Trailing Stop Orders

Trailing stop orders are utilized to protect your capital gains and minimize your losses. This involves setting a stop price, which is a percentage of a stock's current market price or a spread in points. To illustrate, let us say that you have chosen to buy 500 shares from PepsiCo for $50 per share. The price per share now is $57. Your goal is to lock in at least $5 from the per-share profit, but still intent on holding the stock, believing that its share price will still increase in the future. To meet your objective, you decide to place a trailing stop order at $2 per share. At the time your trailing order was placed, your broker knew that, if the price fell below $55 ($57 - $2), he or she could sell your shares. However, if PepsiCo's share price ends up increasing to $62 per share, your trailing order is set to take effect. That is, it gets converted to a market order for a sale price of $60 ($62 - $2). From the market order, you stand to profit $10 per share ($60 - $50).

Bracketed Orders

Bracketed orders are like trailing stop orders, only this time, you add an upper limit to the trailing stop order. So, using the example above, you have placed a bracketed order with a trailing stop order of $2 and impose an upper limit of $65 per share. What happens then is that the order will follow the same tread as that of the trailing stop order. However, given the bracketed order, when PepsiCo's share price reaches $65 per share, then your order will automatically convert to a market order. As you can see, you stand to profit $5 more than what you would have made under the trailing stop order.

Day Orders, GTC Orders, and Extended Hours Orders

All stock orders you place must have an expiration date. When the trading day end, all orders are canceled. This especially applies to market orders. However, Good-till-Cancelled or GTC orders remain open until any of these three things occur:

- Orders are filled

- You canceled the order

- The order remained outstanding for 60 calendar days

Now, there are cons associated with GTC orders. For one, you might end up forgetting it. Take note that a lot of things can happen in 60 days. Two, you may end up paying multiple commissions to your broker as your order becomes partially filled. If you are lucky to have your order filled by numerous transactions, your broker will only need to charge you a single commission. Still, some investors prefer to place an order after hours.

A trading day takes place between 8:00 PM of the current day to 8:00 AM the following day. Placing orders after hours offer one advantage: It allows investors to take precautionary or profitable measures in response to corporate news

Chapter 9.

Risk Assessment Management

Topic Covered:

♦ A Closer Look at Risk Management

♦ Risk is Not Bad

♦ Recommended Risk Management Approach

♦ Risk vs. Reward Ratio

Risk management refers to the entire process of managing risks. Risks are inherent when trading and investing in the markets. It involves assessment, management, and loss prevention activities. Risk management is any action taken by an investor or even a trader to prevent losses. For instance, a trader may buy government-issued bonds that are considered extremely safe.

This is a risk management approach to investing as the trader greatly reduces any potential for losses. If the trader had invested the fund in securities such as stock options or futures, the investment would have been highly risky. Risk management takes place almost always, like when an investor or fund manager decides to adjust to minimize or prevent any inherent risks.

Risk management could be as simple as purchasing one security instead of another, or it could be a rather complex process.

Think about traders who venture into complex securities such as futures and derivatives. Such instruments require serious risk management techniques as these complex securities are highly risky, even though they are also highly rewarding when successful.

A Closer Look at Risk Management

Every trader must consider risk management to avert possible losses in their trades. Without risk management, then traders and investors would just as well resort to gambling. Risk assessment and management ensure enough steps are taken to prevent losses. There are great examples in the recent history of poor risk management approach that led to hundreds of billions in losses incurred by investors. Here we are discussing the collapse of the housing sector in 2007/2008 in the United States. Plenty of homeowners and mortgage holders across the country lost their investments due to the subprime mortgage collapse. This collapse led to the great recession that followed that. It took the US a couple of years to recover from this catastrophe, which also affected other sectors. The entire problem was a result of investments without proper risk management solutions.

Risk is Not Necessarily a Negative Thing

People tend to think of risk as a bad thing. They view it negatively and think of ways of shunning it. Risk does not have to be viewed in negative or derogatory terms. It is a good thing and can save investors and traders from losing their resources.

A lot of investors tend to define investment risk simply as a deviation or variation from an expected result. However, some of the most successful traders engage in very risky investments. The payoff is that they take the time to weigh the risks and even take measures to protect their investments.

Good examples are options and futures traders. Options and futures are considered high risk yet high reward investments. If these investments and trading strategies were extremely risky, then nobody would touch them. However, some focus solely on these highly risky ventures, yet they are the most successful and profitable. As an advanced trader, you need to be able to implement appropriate risk management techniques so that your trades are safe and secure.

One crucial factor that traders need to keep in mind is their appetite for risk. How much risk is one able to take? An investor's appetite for risk will determine his or her strategy as well as the relevant risk-mitigating measures. This way, it will be possible to invest securely with little worry should things not work out as desired. Risk management is essential if you wish to make money in the markets for the long term. Even if you are a great trader and profitable most of the time, your profits can be wiped out in seconds without proper risk management. Risk assessment can be defined as a general term that measures the chances of the likelihood of incurring losses when trading. Risk management also helps to realize the required rate of return so that a strategy becomes successful. As a trader, you need to incorporate risk management as part of your trading strategy. There are many different approaches to risk management, so it is advisable to consider the approach that best works for you.

Recommended Risk Management Approach

1. Plan your trades

The single most crucial aspect of your trade should be risk management. Without it, your whole trading life will be in jeopardy. Therefore, start all your trading ventures with a plan that you intend to stick by. Traders have a saying that you should plan your trades and then trade your plan. This means to come up with the best plan possible and then implement it and stick by it. Trade is very similar to war. When it is well planned, it can be won before it is executed. Some of the best tools you will need as part of your risk management plan are take-profit and stop-loss. Using these two tools, you can plan your trades. You will need to use technical analysis to determine these two points.

2. The One Percent Rule

Traders often apply what is known as the one percent rule. This rule dictates that you should not risk amounts greater than one percent of your total trading capital on one single trade. For instance, if you have $15,000 as your trading capital, you should never risk more than $150 on a single trade. This is a great risk management approach that you can use as part of your trading strategy. Most traders who adopt this strategy have amounts of less than $100,000 in their trading accounts. Some are so more confident, so they choose to work with 2% instead.

3. Set Target and Stops

We can define a stop-loss as the total amount of loss that a trader is willing to incur in a single trade. Beyond the stop-loss point, the trader exits the trade. This is meant to prevent further losses by thinking the trade will eventually get some momentum. Collect any profits made and possibly exit a trade. At this point, stock or other security is often very close to the point of resistance. Beyond this point, a reversal in price is likely to take place. Rather than losing money, you should exit the trade. Traders sometimes take profit and let trade continue if it was still making money. Another take-profit point is then plotted. If you have a good run, you can lock in the profits and let the good run continue.

4. Use of Moving Averages

The best way to identify these two crucial points is to use moving averages. The reason why we prefer moving averages to determine the stop-loss and take-profit points—These are closely tracked by the markets and very simple to determine. Some of the popular moving averages include the 5-day, 20-day, 50-day, 100-day, and 200-day averages. Simply apply these to your security's chart, then decide about the best points. You can also use support and resistance lines to determine the take-profit and stop-loss points. This is also a pretty simple process. Simply connect past lows and highs that happened in the recent past on key, high-than-normal volume levels. All you need to do is find levels where the price action will respond to the trend line on areas of high volume.

Assessing Risk versus Reward

Most traders lose a lot of money at the markets for a very simple reason. They do not know about risk management or how to go about it. This mostly happens to beginners or novice traders. Most of them simply learn how to trade, then rush to the markets in the hope of making a kill. Sadly, this is now how things work because account and risk management are not taken into consideration. Managing risk is just as important as learning how to trade profitably. It is a skill that every trader needs to learn, including beginners and novice traders. As it is, investing hard-earned funds at the markets can be a risky venture. Even with the very best techniques and latest software programs, you can still lose money. Experts also lose money at the markets occasionally. The crucial aspect is that they win a lot more than they lose, so the net equation is profitability.

Since trading is a risky affair, traders should be handsomely compensated for the risks they take. This is where the term risk vs.

reward ratio comes in. If you are going to invest your money in a venture that carries some risk, then it is good to understand the nature of the risk. If it is too risky, you may want to keep away, but if not, then perhaps the risk is worth it.

Steps to Determine a Suitable Risk vs. Reward Ratio

- Identify the most appropriate stock or other security to trade. Make sure that you conduct exhaustive and thorough research to identify the most appropriate security.

- Determine the upside points as well as the downside points. The upside is where you take profit before a reversal while the downside is where you exit a trade to prevent further losses. Use the current price to make these determinations.

- Determine the risk versus reward ratio. Have a threshold for this, and do not take anything below your threshold. Most traders prefer ratios starting at 4:1, even though 2:1 is considered the minimum ratio for any trade. Should your ratio be insufficient, then raise your stop-loss levels to acceptable levels.

Always ensure to apply the risk versus reward ratio for all your trades. Keep in mind the indicated acceptable levels. If you are unable to find acceptable ratios after trying several times, find another security. Once you learn how to incorporate risk management into your trades, you will become safer as you trade without incurring any huge losses.

Chapter 10.

Right Tools to Trade Profitably

Topic Covered:

♦ 6 Right Tools to Trade Profitably

To make sound decisions, you need to base them on solid fundamentals. Some financial models can help you evaluate the performance of a company. Upon proper evaluation, you can determine if the stock is right or take a pass on it until its fundamentals improve.

These models are based on quantitative analysis. Much like technical analysis, quantitative analysis refers to basing decisions on the number and measurable data. While your instincts are important, it is data-driven analytics that will give you the peace of mind that you need when making an investment decision. You can be confident that you made the right call based on the analytics you have used to base your investment decisions.

Tool #1: The Three-Statement Model

This model lives up to its name. It is based on the company's financial statements. Hence, the name "three statement model" refers exactly to this type of model. To conduct the right analysis, you will need to have the following financial statements: balance sheet, profit and loss, and cash flow statement. In this model, what you are doing is essentially linking all three statements to make sense of the company's financial situation. You can use this model to get an accurate idea of a company's overall financial position. If the numbers show health financials, you can feel that the company is in good shape and will produce good results down the road.

Now, the way this model works is to find a way to link all three statements into one model. What you can do is take the trend of each statement and look at how they all move together. If all three statements show a trend for growth, you can be sure that the company is in good shape.

However, if one of the balance sheets is growing, but the profit and loss and the cash flow show signs of trending in the opposite direction, you need to figure out why this is happening. There could be some unexpected situations, but the company is still solid.

If the company is posting profits, but their balance sheet is taking a hit, you can assume that their financials are out of whack. In this case, you would have to evaluate if this investment is worth it. Perhaps it might, but a very short-term deal. The use of this model is perfect for value investing and identifying the potential for a turnaround in a company that's been underwater in recent history.

Tool #2: Initial Public Offering Model

An initial public offering (IPO) is the even in which a company switches from being a private company to be a publicly traded company. In this event, the company is valued at a certain price per share by its financial team. Then the IPO is underwritten by the bank or investment firm, which is essentially sponsoring the IPO.

The issue here is determining the right IPO. This is based on the company's book value, and then a comparative analysis is conducted on the IPOs of similar companies to see where your valuation can fit in.

When you conduct your comparative analysis, you need to consider a set of variables that can be compared among companies. For example, you can compare revenue, gross sales, number of employees, annual turnover, growth rate, and so on.

The actual variables which will be considered can all be compared in a large spreadsheet. Then, each variable can be contrasted with the comparably sized companies so that you can visualize if the results obtained correspond to the comparable.

If you find that your company is above the variables seen in most comparable, then you might be able to value your company at a higher per-share price. If you see that it is below, you might want to reconsider going public. You might want to hold off going public at that time and wait until the company's financials improve.

Now, as an investor, the IPO valuation model is very useful since it allows you to see how individual companies stack against each other. This allows you to determine if your choice to invest in an IPO will make sense for you, or if you're better off waiting for the stock to prove it in the market first.

Investors who get into the early stages of an IPO can make good gains. This can happen when you understand the comparison of that company's IPO. You can see if the valuation makes sense, or if it's being valued too high. In which, you might want to wait to see what happens in the market first. If you see that the valuation is below comparable, you might be looking at a potential bargain.

Tool #3: The Revenue Model

This model consists of charting a company's revenue over a given period to see the trends in that company's revenue.

You can build a model for each company you are interested in trading based on its revenue.

The best way to build this model is to take its historical revenue reports, chart them, and then calculate its trend line. You can do this on commercially available software such as Microsoft Excel, although your brokerage firm may offer you this type of analytics, so you won't have to calculate it yourself.

So, how can you interpret this model?

Once you have charted the historical data for a company's revenue, you can then look at its trend and determine if it is growing or declining. Look at 10 years' worth of data since it will give you an accurate picture of where the company is going. This would be 10 years of quarterly reports. That means that you could have 40 different data points where you can contrast the company's trend. With this model, you can see if the company is expanding, leveling off, or declining. When you see that a company's revenue is growing, you might consider it to be in an expansion phase.

Depending on the age of the company, it could still be developing as part of its growth phase. If the company has been in the market for a longer period, say at least 50 years, you may want to take a look at older data, for example, 25 years, and see if the company is having a renaissance due to factors such as management turnover, the introduction of new products, or a shift in market conditions.

This model is simple since it only looks at the behavioral patterns of one variable over time, but it is the most powerful variable in stock trading.

You can then overlay a company's revenue trend line with that of other economic variables such as Gross Domestic Product (GDP), inflation, consumer confidence, and major stock indices to see if the company is responding to the factors around it, or it is producing results despite the trends observed in the overall economy.

The best part of this model is that you can overlay as many variables as you like to get a sense of where that company's revenue is going as compared to any number of variables in its surroundings.

Tool #4: The Forecasting Model

Industry experts will produce forecasts for companies' revenue.

These forecasts respond to the available data that analysts are looking at when determining where a company's earnings report should fall. These forecasts will produce an actual Dollar figure, which estimates where that company's earnings report should fall.

Usually, forecasting is done on an earnings per share basis. This means that the per earnings per share price are calculated based on that company's track record and other variables that can be taken into accounts, such as economic conditions affecting it and any other variables which may come into play.

From that, analysts will produce a forecast where they expect that company's earnings per share to fall in line. This is where analysts' expectations are bred. If the company beats analysts' expectations,

STOCK MARKET INVESTING STRATEGIES

Tool #5: Resistance Level Model

This model takes the trend in moving averages to determine where "resistance" levels can be found. A found resistance level is a psychological barrier that investors and traders must pass to continue with the stock trend. Resistance levels are seen both at the top and the bottom, that is, both the floor and the ceiling of a stock.

If a stock is trending upward, you may often see that it won't pass a certain point. This would be a resistance level. It is often hard for a stock to break through a resistance level because investors may not feel comfortable paying a certain price above a previous high.

To determine resistance levels, you need to look at the candlesticks of a stock and compare it to its overall trend at the different points for moving averages. It could be that the 10-day moving average is trading in each range, but it is not surpassing the high point of the 200-day moving average.

You can choose to approach the stock in many ways when you are in the presence of a resistance level.

First, you can choose today to trade the stock within that range. You can set up a buy order when the price falls to the lowest point you have observed in its 10-day or 50-day trend. Then, you can set up your sell order when it hits the resistance level ceiling. This strategy can help you make some decent if underwhelming profits. But if the stock doesn't break the resistance level, you can feel confident about trading within that range.

Tool #6: The Gap up Model

When stocks close on high at the end of a trading day, investors may be looking to continue pushing the stock upward at the opening of the following trading day. This is common when a company's report data in the afternoon of a trading day.

As such, investors may choose to wait until the following trading day to pursue this stock. As a savvy day trader, you can purchase the stock right at the beginning of the trading day and wait for the gap to fill. When you hear that a "gap is filling," it means that the stock will go back to its previous highs after the euphoria has passed.

Chapter 11.

Trading Full-Time or Part-Time

Topic Covered:

♦ Source of Income

♦ Flexibility

♦ Cost-Effective

♦ Limited Risks ans Losses

♦ Make Huge Profits

♦ Less Commission

♦ Liquidity and Profits Even with Low Investment

Trading to get long term profits is called longer-term position trading. This is different from the shorter-term scalping that is day trading. If you want to head into this direction, then it is imperative you get familiar with some strategies to achieve success. You need to know that the amount of money you inject into this venture is not going to come back in a short time, and you must, therefore, be very ready to make that investment. Below are some benefits of trading:

Source of Income

Financial independence is the dream of every individual. Day trading can easily get you this freedom. A trader can trade as many times as they can in a single day. Depending on how good they can trade, they can earn huge profits from the trades that they engage in.

The main trick to becoming a good investor depends on how well an investor can utilize the various option strategies to earn a source of income. For you to become an expert trader, you need to have some tactics that you can utilize. Those tactics set you apart from the novice traders. You might be wondering how you can get to this point while you are just getting started.

Flexibility

We can describe flexibility in two ways. The first way is the fact that you can trade anywhere at any preferred time, and you can engage in any trade you would like. Most people do not get this, and that's why they make conclusions that options trading is a scam. Well, it is not as easy as it may seem.

One must use our mind and spend some time learning more about how it works. It is an investment that you can easily engage in and earn your profits at the end of the day if you know how to do it right. The other way is the fact that once a trader purchases an option, they can trade as many times as they can to earn a profit.

Insurance

Options contracts can be utilized for insurance purposes. For a trader to use an option contract as insurance, they must build a good portfolio. Your portfolio indicates the profits an individual has made, together with the losses. A good portfolio needs to have more profits and fewer losses. As you trade, you need to ensure that you master the art of trading options.

This involves using the right trading plan and strategies to maximize your profits. Building a good portfolio is not a hard task. It is something that you can easily accomplish if you are committed to what you do. You keep getting better at it with every day that passes.

In the beginning, you may encounter some challenges, but do not allow them to prevent you from getting where you would like to get.

It is also important for you as a beginner to trust the process and believe that you will make it at the end of it all. Once you establish a good portfolio, you can use it as your insurance. It ensures that you do not acquire a complete loss in case a trade goes contrary to what you expected.

Cost-Effective

Different options contracts are priced differently. We have some that are more expensive than others. There are several factors that we must consider when it comes to pricing options.

Some of these factors include; the strike price, stock price, dividends, underlying asset, and the expiry date. When it comes to the expiry date, the options contracts that have a short period before they expire tend to have low prices. On the other hand, the options contracts, whose expiry date is quite far, tend to be highly-priced.

Limited Losses

Don't think you can make money within a short period of time, without having a strategy. You cannot invest blindly and still expect an income at the end of the day. A lot of effort, commitment, and dedication will be needed. Most people miss this fact, and that is why they end up making losses.

Once they have incurred the losses, they conclude that day trading is a scam. We have had most of the traders engage in overtrading only to end up losing every penny that they have invested. To avoid this, one must be aware of the various option strategies. The different strategies are all aimed at increasing profits and reducing the losses. This is easily achievable if one is committed to learning how each strategy works and when to utilize each best.

Limited Risks

If you know much about investments, then you understand that most businesses, deals, or trades people engage in having risks. There is no single investment that an individual can engage in and fail to encounter risks. Day trading is no different from other investments. At times, you will have to be open to the possibility of encountering some risks. If not controlled, it can result in fewer profits or no profit at all.

Before engaging in a trade, evaluate all the possible risks. Get to know which you can afford to minimize as you live aside those that you have no control over. You need the right option strategy to do so. Depending on the type of trade you chose to undertake, you can easily get a suitable strategy to utilize.

The strategy needs to be effective in minimizing the risks so you can earn more profits. As a trader, ensure you are aware of all the option strategies that you can utilize in a trade. This knowledge allows you to make the right decisions while trading, and you easily earn profits as you reduce the potential risks.

Make Huge Profits

Every investor aspires to earn profits from the investments that they make. With day trading, you can make your dreams come true. One of the good things about day trading is that you can trade multiple times.

As you engage in different trades, it is good to keenly observe what you do to ensure that you avoid making wrong decisions. Ensure that you evaluate all the trades that you engage in.

This allows you to evaluate the possibility of incurring a loss or a profit. You get to know the trades that you can engage in and those that you need to avoid. As a beginner, avoid the trades with a high possibility of earning a loss and, at the same time, have a high possibility of earning huge profits. Such trade may seem to be good, especially if you lean on the possibility of earning huge profits.

However, do not forget that both possibilities are applicable, and you can also make a huge loss. In such cases, you will be required to make the right decisions that can result in you earning profits. You can also deal with multiple trades that earn small profits and get a huge profit at the end of the day.

Less Commission

Less commission means that you earn more profits. While selecting the best brokerage account to use while trading, this is one of the factors you will have to consider. Ensure that the brokerage account has fewer commissions so you can increase your income. Different accounts have different rates for their services. As you do your research, you will come across some accounts with high commissions and those with low commissions.

If you go with the accounts with high commissions, it will affect your profit. You will find that a percentage of your profits will be slashed and go into catering for the high commissions. Avoid such accounts and work with those that have low commission.

As a beginner, you need to properly analyze all your choices to come up with the best solution. It's a good thing that with a single click, you can get all the information you would like from the internet. The analysis given in various brokerage accounts can also help you identify the various services that they provide and their rates.

Liquidity

At the end of a trade, some traders like seeing the impact of their efforts on investing. Liquidity refers to the process in which an asset can be converted into cash. Upon investing in options trading, you can earn your money.

As the holder of an option, you can exercise your contract and get paid depending on the payment method in the brokerage account. While opening a brokerage account, some accounts will require that you fill in your bank details.

This information will be useful while buying and selling options. In some accounts, you can fill in your E-wallet details. In case you have a PayPal account, your payment can be credited or debited from your account. We have some accounts that utilize cryptocurrencies. You find that a trader can use bitcoins to sell or buy a 55 options contract.

Profits Even with Low Investment

You may find it difficult to invest a lot in an investment that you are new to. The good thing about options trading is that you can invest in any amount you would like.

Earlier on, I stated that options are priced differently. I also explained the factors that influence the pricing of options. You find that you can easily find cheap and affordable options contracts that you can engage in.

Chapter 12.

Different Types of Securities

Topic Covered:

♦ Securities

♦ Stocks

♦ Bonds

♦ Options and Derivatives

♦ Currencies

There are numerous types of securities out there. In finance, we define security as a tradable financial asset. This means the financial asset can be traded, bought, or sold, at the financial markets.

Securities are crucial for the global financial system. Some financial instruments are created to afford their owners a variety of options. This means anyone with a financial tool can sell, purchase, hold, assume or relinquish ownership, and so much more

There are specific securities that are traded more than others. Day traders generally prefer certain securities. These include stocks, currencies, and contracts for difference. Others are futures contrasts like commodity futures, currency futures, interest rate futures, and equity index futures.

Securities

These are financial instruments traded on exchanges around the globe. Some of these popular exchanges include the London Stock Exchange, New York Stock Exchange, and exchanges in cities such as Hong Kong, Tokyo, Paris, and Sydney.

Some securities, such as bonds and other fixed-income assets are traded across the secondary markets. There are millions of individuals around the world who hold various securities, especially stocks, bonds, and others. Other entities include exchange-traded funds or ETFs and mutual funds.

Before security is made available to the public, it must be vetted. The regulator must assess large firms and corporations that wish to list at the stock market to raise money for different purposes. In the US, this regulator is the SEC or securities exchange commission.

The stock and bond markets are also referred to as capital markets. Companies need to seek funds from the public list at the markets so that individuals and institutions purchase their stocks and then trade them back and forth whenever they want.

Large companies must liaise with investment bankers and underwriters to help in the preparation of listing their securities at the markets. These securities could be bonds, stocks, and so on. The investment bankers will generally examine the company's financial position and the amount it intends to raise. It is based on this that the firm will likely recommend the number of shares or securities to be issued and how to approach the entire listing process.

Stocks and bonds are generally the most common and best-known types of financial securities available. They are also the most commonly traded securities, together with a few others. However, they are not the only financial instruments traded at the capital markets. We also have options, derivatives, indexes, currencies, warrants, and debentures, and even US Treasury securities.

All these securities have a few things in common. They all carry a certain value that makes them admirable to both traders and investors. However, the risk profiles of these securities vary greatly. Different traders and investors have different risk appetites. Therefore, the choice of security to trade or invest in varies.

Take bonds and stocks, for instance. Stocks carry a higher risk level compared to bonds because of how they respond to market fluctuations and the general economic state. Bonds are a lot more stable even though the income they provide is considered fixed.

Stocks

By far, stocks are the most popular form of security sold and purchased by traders and investors at the markets. There are different kinds of stocks, such as ordinary shares. These are sold to the public by the parent company through the stock market. Stocks from very successful companies that are profitable over the years are referred to as blue-chip stocks.

We also have internal stocks as well as niche-specific stocks. Common stocks regularly transacted at exchanges are also known as equities. The reason why stocks are by far the most popular sort of security traded is that they have the highest return. Stocks, on average, have a return of 9.2%. In comparison, bonds have seen a return of about 6.5% within the same 50-year period.

Bonds

Another popular security that is common among day traders is the bond. Bonds are ideally a form of investment where investors put their money in debt, either public or private. Therefore, bonds are largely considered to be instruments of debt.

Bonds are also known as debt securities, so a trader who deals in bonds is purchasing a debt instrument. Compare this to traders who deal in stocks, which are essentially units of ownership of a listed company.

Companies or organizations that issue bonds often do so to raise money for a certain financial obligation. For instance, governments may issue a bond to expand or improve the local infrastructure. At the same time, companies do so to expand into new markets or sometimes even to come up with a new product line and similar ventures. Banks also issue instruments like bonds.

These are known as certificates of deposit. Banks issue these to receive funds they need most to lend to their customers. Investors or buyers of certificates of deposit, often received a certain fixed rate of interest for their investment. Certificates of deposit are short-term investment tools used by banks to raise revenue for their operations.

Options and Derivatives

Another common type of security is a derivative. Derivatives are financial securities whose value is directly related to an underlying security. This means the price is derived from the price of the underlying asset and hence the term derivative.

A good example of derivatives is an options contract. Equity options contracts are contracts between a buyer and a seller regarding an underlying asset. The asset is most cases are most often stocks. Not many retail traders deal in options, but numerous professional traders trade-in options regularly. Others include investment firms, commercial and investment banks, hedge funds, and other companies that need to balance their portfolios.

At the most basic level, equity options contract that award buyers a right to sell or purchase underlying stocks at a certain price and within a certain period. It is important to note that this is a right, but not an obligation. Beginner and novice traders should generally stay as far away from derivatives as possible because they are extremely risky.

Currencies

Trade-in currencies are sometimes referred to as Forex or foreign exchange. It involves the purchase and sale of currencies at an exchange. The main aim of currency trading is to make a profit. The gist behind currency trading is that currency prices fluctuate, and based on these fluctuations, and traders can capitalize and earn a profit.

There is a reason why some day traders prefer trading currencies. One reason is that the currency market is the largest in the entire world. This market has a turnover of $2 trillion every single day. This is massive even when compared to other large securities markets such as NYSE.

Conclusion

Start practicing your stock trading skills, stock market analysis, applying different strategies, and using various financial tools, including chart reading. All these are simple and straightforward. If you put your heart and mind to it, you will get to learn and understand how the stock markets function eventually.

It is impressive to learn that buying and selling stocks is a pretty simple affair. Most traders and investors, including novices, can pull this off. The main challenge will be to learn how to choose the winners. There are quite several stocks in all the different industries and sectors of the economy. If you learn how to identify the winning stocks, then you can expect your investments to grow immensely over the years.

A lot of investors across America and elsewhere worldwide have managed to create wealth for themselves and their families through stock market investments. You, too, can achieve this success through prudent investments over time.

There are different strategies and approaches to stock market investing. If you can find the right approach and be committed to the strategy you choose, you will enjoy long term success. Remember to start investing as soon as possible because the sooner you start, the better off you will be. Investing in the stock market can seem confusing when you are first starting. If you have tried to learn about investing only to find yourself more confused than before, don't feel bad. There is so much complex information about investing in the stock market that it can make investing seem unattainable.

While many people want to overcomplicate investing in the stock market, I have good news for you. None of it is necessary. By investing in index funds and allowing your investment to grow over a long period, you will be able to grow your wealth while avoiding all the overcomplicated information.

Swing trading allows short financial motion in unequivocally slanting stocks to ride the wave toward the example. Swing exchanging merges the best of two universes—the more moderate pace of contributing and the extended potential increments of day exchanging.

Swing vendors hold stocks for an impressive period or weeks playing the general upward or plunging designs. Swing Trading isn't fast day exchanging. A couple of individuals call it waves, contributing considering the way that you simply hold puts that are making basic moves. By turning your money over rapidly through transient expands, you can quickly build up your worth.

The basic procedure of Swing trading is to dip into an unequivocally inclining stock after its season of company or remedy is done.

A swing trader will most likely make money by getting the quick moves that stocks make in their future and all the while controlling their risk by proper means of the managers' methodologies.

Swing trading joins the best of two universes—the more moderate pace of contributing and the extended potential augmentations of day exchanging. Swing trading capacities splendidly for low support vendors—especially those doing it while at work.

While day traders' wager on stocks popping or falling by divisions of centers, swing traders endeavor to ride "swings" in the market. Swing traders buy less shares and go for dynamically basic augmentations, they pay lower business and, theoretically, have an unrivaled probability of gaining progressively immense increments.

With day exchanging, the principle individual getting rich is the mediator. "Swing vendors go for the meat of the move while a casual investor just gets scraps." Furthermore, to swing exchanging, you don't need refined PC catch ups or lightning smart execution organizations, and you don't have to play entirely erratic stocks.

Swing exchanging is a splendid methodology used by various sellers transversely over various markets. It isn't simply used in the Forex trade, yet it is a crucial mechanical assembly in prospects and financial markets.

Financial experts will, when all is said in done, have a progressively broadened term time horizon and are not generally impacted by fleeting financial changes. Swing exchanging is only a solitary framework and should be utilized exactly when appropriately grasped. Like any exchanging strategies, swing exchanging can be risky, and a moderate approach can change into day exchanging systems quickly. If you mean to use a swing exchanging system, ensure that you totally appreciate the risks and develop a method that will presumably empower you to create more prominent rate returns on your positions.

Index funds are a great investment for people who don't have the time to go out and learn everything they know about the stock market. You can think of an index fund as a set it and forget it system. When you invest in an index fund, you don't let the market's inevitable fluctuations pull you from your course. Instead, you leave your investment, continue to add to it, and allow it to grow as the market begins to rise again.

By doing this, you will take all the emotions out of investing, and you will be setting yourself up with a nice little nest egg for the future.

With all this insight, you should be able to successfully carry out a trade from start to finish. You must, however, note that the options business is not for every investor.

By now, it is clear to you whether this is an investment you want to try out or not. If you are into it, you must decide the kind of trader you want to be. You can either be a day trader, long term trader, or a short-term trader. As a day trader, you will have the advantage of making several trades that close quickly. This option is good for you if you are interested in making small profits. Otherwise, consider long-term trading that can span over 30 days, but with incredible profits.

Nothing will replace your raw experience when it comes to running this kind of business. As I mentioned before, the best way to gain experience is through experience. The best way to learn how to ride a bike is to work on riding a bike. You must do, and you must try to make progress. The best way to learn how to drive a car is by driving a car.

It is important to note that the shorter the trading period, the higher the stress and risks involved. If you keep holding your trades through the night, you stand a high risk of losing all your capital and destroying your account. Other than this, we are glad that you have learned a new way of earning money from the financial market and understood all the traits and skills you need to make it in binary options trading. Note that theory is never effective without practice.

So, in case you need to get started, it is best to identify a trading platform and put what you have learned into practice. Remember, the more you practice, the more confident you become.

Dave R. W. Graham

A Gift for You

If you enjoyed this book and you want to have a complete guide on stock market investments, and trading strategies (including Swing and Day trading) then you will be interested in the complete collection of our author:

INVESTING AND TRADING STRATEGIES:
The Complete Crash Course with Proven Strategies to Become a Profitable Trader in the Financial Markets and Stop Living Paycheck to Paycheck.

If you love listening to audio books on-the-go, I have great news for you.

You Can Download the Audio Book Version of This Collection for FREE:

This audiobook is the complete box set of 11 books in the "Investing and trading Academy" series. They are collected in 4 main books: Stock Market Investing, Options Trading, Swing, and Day Trading Strategies. It can be yours for FREE.

Just by signing up for a FREE 30-day audible trial! See below for more details!

- FREE audible book copy of this book
- After the trial, you will get 1 credit each month to use on any audiobook
- Your credits automatically roll over to the next month if you don't use them
- Choose from Audible's 200,000 + titles
- Listen anywhere with the Audible app across multiple devices
- Make easy, no-hassle exchanges of any audiobook you don't love
- Keep your audiobooks forever, even if you cancel your membership

… and much more

Just scan the QR code below with your smartphone to get started right now FOR FREE!

For Audible US

For Audible UK

For Audible FR

For Audible DE

IPH BOOKS
INVESTING AND TRADING ACADEMY

Other Author's Works

by IPH Books - "Investing and trading Academy" Series

Stock Market Investing for Beginners

The Complete and Quick Guide to Becoming a Smart, Millionaire Investor by Recognizing the Best Investments. Learn How to Build and Diversify Your Investment Portfolio and Increase Your Wealth.

Stock Market Investing Strategies:

Complete and Quick Guide to Finding Out the Best Investment Strategies for Beginners, to Make Your First Passive Income and to Master the Financial Markets without Fear.

Forex Trading for Beginners:

A Quick Guide to Find Out How to Make Money in Few Weeks Mastering Forex, CFD, Commodities, and Cryptocurrencies Markets with Simple Swing and Day Trading Strategies.

Options Trading for Beginners:

A Quick Guide to Learn How to Use Options to Beat the Stock Markets, and Protect Your Investment, even if You Have a Small Capital, Using Leverage.

Options Trading Strategies:

The Proven Guide to Increase Your Credit Score Once and For All. Manage Your Money, Your Personal Finance, And Your Debt to Achieve Financial Freedom Effortlessly.

Technical Analysis for Your Profitable Trading:

A complete and quick guide for beginners to learn all you need to master financial markets with charting and technical analysis.

Swing Trading for Beginners:

Simple Quick Guide to Learn How to Manage Your Trading Positions in Different Markets. Find Out How to Build Your Profitable Swing Trading Plan and Avoid Common Mistakes.

Swing Trading Strategies:

Discover proven and effective strategies to profit from swing trading, get a passive income and maximize your gains.

Day Trading for Beginners:

Everything You Need to Start Making Money Daily Right Away. Find Out All the Basics and Tips and Tricks to Become a Successful Day Trader.

Day trading Strategies:

A Quick Start Guide to Learning Technical Analysis and Becoming a Profitable Trader. Find Out Tips and Tricks with Simple Strategies to Build Your Next Passive Income Day-by-Day.

Trading for a Living:

A Complete Guide for Beginners and Intermediates on Money Management, Risk, Discipline, and the Psychology of Successful Trading. Everything You Need to Know to Get a Guaranteed Income for Life.

IPH BOOKS
INVESTING AND TRADING ACADEMY

by IPH Books - "Wealth Management Academy" Series

Credit Secrets: 3 Book in 1, Including An Unpublished Work:

The Complete Guide To Finding Out All the Secrets To Fix Your Credit Report and Boost Your Score. Learn How To Improve Your Finances and Have a Wealthy Lifestyle.

Credit Score Secrets

The Proven Guide To Increase Your Credit Score Once And For All. Manage Your Money, Your Personal Finance, And Your Debt To Achieve Financial Freedom Effortlessly.

Credit Repair Secrets:

Learn the Strategies and Techniques of Consultants and Credit Attoneys to Fix your Bad Debt and Improve your Business or Personal Finance. Including Dispute Letters.

IPH BOOKS
INVESTING AND TRADING ACADEMY

Author's Note

Thanks for reading my book. If you want to learn more about personal finance, investments, trading, and business, I suggest you follow my author page on Amazon. Through my books, I have decided to share with you the know-how that has allowed me to achieve my financial freedom, to accumulate wealth, and to live the life I want with my family.

My goal is to show you the path for reaching your targets, with useful and applicable information. Only you will be able to tread that path as I did... and now, I'm sharing what I know.

To your wealth!

Dave R. W. Graham

CPSIA information can be obtained
at www.ICGtesting.com
Printed in the USA
LVHW080215180621
690358LV00023B/304